— THE UNTOLD STORY OF —
SYLVIA MENDEZ
SCHOOL DESEGREGATION PIONEER

BY LETICIA GONZALES

Consultant:
Dr. Jimmy Patiño
Associate Professor
Department of Chicano & Latino Studies
University of Minnesota, Twin Cities

CAPSTONE PRESS
a capstone imprint

Published by Capstone Press, an imprint of Capstone
1710 Roe Crest Drive, North Mankato, Minnesota 56003
capstonepub.com

Library of Congress Cataloging-in-Publication Data is available on the Library of Congress website.
ISBN: 9781669005049 (hardcover)
ISBN: 9781669004998 (paperback)
ISBN: 9781669005001 (ebook PDF)

Summary: You probably know that the 1954 *Brown v. Board of Education* case was an important part of ending segregation in schools. But it wasn't the only one. In 1947, *Mendez v. Westminster* helped end segregation in California schools. Uncover Mendez's story and how it connects to *Brown v. Board of Education*.

Editorial Credits
Editor: Ericka Smith; Designer: Sarah Bennett; Media Researcher: Svetlana Zhurkin; Production Specialist: Katy LaVigne

Image Credits
Alamy: Abaca Press/Olivier Douliery, 28; Getty Images: Corbis/Dick Whittington Studio, 13; Granger: 11; Library of Congress: Prints and Photographs Division, 21, 25, Prints and Photographs Division/U.S. Farm Security Administration/ Dorothea Lange, 7; National Archives and Records Administration: 18; Newscom: Zuma Press/Ana Venegas, 5, 17, Zuma Press/Cindy Yamanaka, 23; San Diego History Center: 15; Shutterstock: Julia Khimich (background), cover (right) and throughout, Nadegda Rozova (background), cover (left) and throughout; The University of Texas at Austin: The Dolph Briscoe Center for American History/ Russell Lee Photograph Collection (e_rl_14646_0038), 8; U.S. Army Corps of Engineers: Richard Rivera, cover, 27

Direct Quotations
Page 9, from March 11, 2016, *Latino USA* article, "'No Mexicans Allowed:' School Segregation in the Southwest," latinousa.org
Page 28, from April 17, 2016, *Los Angeles Times* article, "Mendez vs. Segregation: 70 Years Later, Famed Case 'Isn't Just about Mexicans. It's about Everybody Coming Together,'" latimes.com

All internet sites appearing in back matter were available and accurate when this book was sent to press.

Printed and bound in the USA. 5195

TABLE OF CONTENTS

Words in **bold** are in the glossary.

BREAKING BARRIERS

In September 1944, eight-year-old Sylvia Mendez went with her aunt, her brothers, and her cousins to 17th Street School in Westminster, California. Her aunt wanted to enroll all of them in the school. Mendez and her brothers were turned away. They were told to enroll at Hoover Elementary School instead. That school was for Mexican and Mexican American children. Her cousins had lighter skin, and their last name was Vidaurri. They could enroll in the all-white school.

Mendez's family thought it was unfair that their children could not attend 17th Street School. Her father, Gonzalo Mendez, spoke to the principal. He also talked to the school board. Neither would allow the Mendez children to attend the school.

Gonzalo didn't give up his fight. He wanted his children to have the same education as white children. So he hired a lawyer and helped build a case against **segregation** in the district's schools.

Mendez (left), her sister, and one of her brothers with a photo of their parents in 2013

That case—*Mendez v. Westminster*—would help end segregation in California schools. It would also help pave the way for *Brown v. Board of Education*, the Supreme Court case that **outlawed** segregation across the country in 1954.

You've probably heard about *Brown v. Board of Education*. This is the story of a student whose case helped make it possible—Sylvia Mendez.

CHAPTER 1

A LATINE FAMILY IN CALIFORNIA

Mendez was born on June 7, 1936, in Santa Ana, California. Her father, Gonzalo, was Mexican. Her mother, Felicitas, was Puerto Rican. In 1944, the Mendez family moved to Westminster, California. There, they leased a farm from a Japanese American family that had been sent to an **internment camp**.

At the time, many **Latine** people in the United States experienced **exploitation** and discrimination. Many Mexican workers were used as cheap labor, especially in **agriculture**. And schools, restaurants, movie theaters, and other places were segregated.

Mexican farmworkers on a cantaloupe farm in California in 1938

A sign outside a restaurant denying service to people of Mexican descent in the late 1940s

Mendez's family experienced discrimination. Once, her family was refused service at a restaurant. "My father, who spoke very good English, said, 'Miss, why aren't we being served?' and the waitress said it was because they didn't serve Mexicans there, so we had to get up and leave," Mendez recalled.

Her family had to use a segregated pool too. They weren't allowed to swim at the same time as white people. They couldn't use the pool until Monday, "when the water was dirty," remembered Mendez. "After we got in the pool, they would take out the water and put new water in for the white children," she explained.

"Mexican Schools" in California

There were no laws that kept children of Mexican descent from attending schools with white children in California. People of Mexican descent were considered white. Instead, as the Mexican American population grew, school districts started creating separate classrooms and schools for them. Often, the need to teach them English and the need to help them adjust to American culture were used as reasons to create separate "Mexican schools."

Teaching children to read and write was not the priority at some Mexican schools. Boys were trained to work as laborers. They were prepared for jobs in agriculture and in **industrial** fields. Girls were taught housekeeping skills, like sewing and knitting.

FACT Many Latine children had trouble with the English language because they weren't actually being taught English at the Mexican schools.

Students at a Spanish-speaking school in New Mexico in the 1940s

Mexican schools were also not as nice as white schools, and students did not have access to the same learning materials. In Westminster, there was a big difference between 17th Street School and Hoover Elementary School. When Mendez went to school, she would get off the bus at the white school. It was a nice school with a playground. She would have to walk the rest of the way to her school. It was two wooden shacks next to a cow pasture. And it had broken desks and old books.

FACT In 1919, school districts in Orange County—where the Mendez family would settle—began to create Mexican schools. Mexican parents in Santa Ana expressed their concerns to the school board, but they were ignored.

Children playing outside an elementary school in California in the early 1930s

A Lawsuit in Lemon Grove, California

On January 5, 1931, the principal of Lemon Grove Grammar School, Jerome T. Green, stopped about 75 Mexican American students from entering the school. He was following instructions from the school board.

Green directed them to a new school. It was a two-room building that had been built for Mexican American students. The students' parents had found out about the plan to segregate their children, so they told their children to return home if they were sent to another school. That's what the students did.

Their parents organized a **boycott** of the school. They found a lawyer and filed a **lawsuit**. The case was called *Roberto Alvarez v. the Board of Trustees of the Lemon Grove School District*. It was the first court decision against school segregation in the United States.

The Mexican American families won that case. The district could no longer segregate children based on their Mexican descent. But the decision in that case only affected the Lemon Grove School District.

Students at Lemon Grove Grammar School around 1928

CHAPTER 2

SYLVIA'S CASE

When the Mendez children were turned away from 17th Street School, Gonzalo was determined to do something about it. Talking to the principal and the school board didn't work. So he decided to take his case to court.

Gonzalo hired attorney David Marcus to help him fight the school district. Gonzalo tried to find families in his community to join the case. But many people in his community liked having the school in their neighborhood.

Gonzalo visited other communities. He found families who'd also had trouble enrolling their children in white schools. Thomas Estrada, William Guzman, Frank Palomino, and Lorenzo Ramirez joined the case.

Lorenzo Ramirez

1   DAVID C. MARCUS.

2   Attorney at Law.

3   212 Spring & Second Bldg.

4   Los Angeles, California.

5   VA. 6311

6

7

8   IN THE DISTRICT COURT OF THE UNITED STATES

9   FOR THE SOUTHERN DISTRICT OF CALIFORNIA

10   CENTRAL DIVISION

11   GONZALO MENDEZ and SYLVIA, GONZALO and

12   GERONIMO MENDEZ, by their father and next
      of friend GONZALO MENDEZ,

13   WILLIAM GUZMAN and BILLY GUZMAN, by his
      father and next of friend WILLIAM GUZMAN,

14   FRANK PALOMINO, and ARTHUR and SALLY
      PALOMINO, by their father and next of friend

15   FRANK PALOMINO,
      THOMAS ESTRADA and CLARA, ROBERTO, FRANCISCO,

16   SYRIA, DANIEL and EVELINA ESTRADA, by their
      father and next of friend, THOMAS ESTRADA,

17   LORENZO RAMIREZ and IGNACIO, SILVERIO and
      JOSE RAMIREZ, by their father and next of

18   friend LORENZO RAMIREZ,

19

20   Petitioners.   PETITION

21   -vs-

22   WESTMINISTER SCHOOL DISTRICT OF ORANGE COUNTY,   No. 4292-M
      and J. A. HOULIHAN, LEWIS CONRADY, RAY SCHMITT,

23   as Trustees and J. HARRIS, Superintendent of
      said School District,

24   GARDEN GROVE ELEMENTARY SCHOOL DISTRICT OF
      ORANGE COUNTY and WILLIAM C. NOBLE, ROBERT B.

25   SMITH and PAUL APPLEBURY as Trustees and
      JAMES L. KENT, Superintendent of said School

26   District,
      SANTA ANA CITY SCHOOLS and GEORGE R. WELLS,

27   HIRAM M. CURREY, JAMES K. GIVENS, DANIEL W.
      STOVER and GEORGE J. BUSDIEKER its Board of

28   Education and FRANK A. HENDERSON and HAROLD
      YOST, its Superintendent and Secretary,

29   EL MODENO SCHOOL DISTRICT and HENRY CAMPBELL,
      THEODORE HOWER, CLARENCE JOHNSON as Trustees,

30   and HAROLD HAMMARSTEN, Superintendent of
      said School District,

31

32   Respondents.

The lawsuit filed in the Mendez case

Marcus filed a lawsuit against four school districts in Orange County. It represented 5,000 Mexican American students. The case was called *Mendez v. Westminster.*

Marcus argued that school segregation violated the Fourteenth Amendment to the U.S. Constitution. The amendment guarantees equal protection under the law. It was unfair to segregate students just because they were of Mexican descent.

Marcus also argued that segregating Mexican American children harmed them. It kept them from learning English and American customs. It also kept them from feeling a sense of belonging in the community. It made them feel **inferior**.

On February 18, 1946, Judge Paul J. McCormick decided in favor of the Mendezes and the other families. There was no law in California that required segregating students of Mexican descent—who were considered white under the law—so the school districts didn't have the right to do so. There were laws about segregating other students, including Black and Indigenous students.

The school districts filed an **appeal**. Many organizations—including the National Association for the Advancement of Colored People (NAACP)—wrote to the court to support the Mexican American families. On April 14, 1947, judges upheld McCormick's ruling. The school districts did not file any more appeals.

Thurgood Marshall and the NAACP

During the Mendez case, Thurgood Marshall was one of the NAACP attorneys watching it closely. At the time, the NAACP had been building legal cases that challenged racial segregation in education, so they were interested in the case. The NAACP even wrote a brief to show support for the Mexican American families during the appeal.

Marcus's legal arguments, that segregation was a violation of the Fourteenth Amendment and that it harmed students, were new ones—and they worked. The success of this case would help Marshall build similar legal arguments in the Supreme Court case *Brown v. Board of Education*.

After the Battle

After the ruling, older children in Westminster went to what had been the Mexican school. Younger children went to what had been the all-white school. Eventually, the school district shut down the former Mexican school because parents complained about its poor condition.

At first, Sylvia Mendez did not want to attend what had been the all-white school. "I was crying and crying, and told my mother, 'I don't want to go to the white school!' And she said, 'Don't you know what we were fighting? We weren't fighting so you could go to that beautiful white school. We were fighting because you're equal to that white boy.'"

Unfortunately, at school Mendez was bullied and treated cruelly by other students.

FACT Even after the Mendez ruling, many schools found other ways to keep Mexican American children from enrolling. One way they did this was by requiring that children take tests in order to keep different groups separated.

A mural in a Santa Ana, California, courthouse that represents the Mendez case

THE CASE'S HISTORIC IMPACT

Mendez's court case helped desegregate schools across California. In June 1947, Governor Earl Warren signed a law that banned school segregation in the state. It also led to desegregation cases in other states. Within a few years, laws that segregated Mexican American students in Texas and Arizona were struck down too.

In December 1952, the NAACP argued their case against segregating Black students before the U.S. Supreme Court in *Brown v. Board of Education*. Thurgood Marshall was one of the attorneys on that case. And Earl Warren was a justice on the Supreme Court by the time it made a decision.

On May 17, 1954, the Supreme Court declared racial segregation in public schools unconstitutional. Their decision overturned the **precedent** set in the 1896 *Plessy v. Ferguson* case, which made segregated facilities legal as long as they were equal.

Brown v. Board of Education Changes the Nation

When the NAACP made its case in *Brown v. Board of Education*, taking on the "separate but equal" precedent set by the 1896 *Plessy v. Ferguson* case was a huge challenge. They were up against more than 50 years of segregation that the U.S. government had allowed. Even in the *Mendez v. Westminster* case, judges were hesitant to address the precedent set in the Plessy case.

The ruling in *Brown v. Board of Education*, though, had a huge impact as a new Supreme Court precedent that directly challenged the ruling in the Plessy case. Not only was it going to change the lives of American students across the country, it was going to help end racial segregation in other places too.

CHAPTER 4

SPEAKING UP AND RECEIVING RECOGNITION

After the court case, Sylvia Mendez went on to graduate from Santa Ana High School. Then, she earned a nursing degree. She spent the next 33 years working as a nurse.

After her father died in 1964, Mendez began thinking about his work to end segregation. When Mendez's mother became ill in 1998, she told Sylvia to continue their fight for equality. After her mother's death, Mendez began traveling and speaking about activism and equality for students. After she retired, she started speaking to students about staying in school.

Mendez speaking in 2011

In recent years, the Mendezes have received recognition for their fight against segregation. Their court case was featured in the 2002 documentary *Mendez vs. Westminster: For All the Children*. In 2004, Mendez was invited to the White House by President George W. Bush during Hispanic Heritage Month. And in 2007, the United States Post Office issued a stamp celebrating her court case.

Mendez received an even greater honor from President Barack Obama. In 2011, he awarded her the Presidential Medal of Freedom. She received it for her work teaching students and others about desegregation in the United States. "When I got it, I couldn't stop crying, because I was thinking finally my mother and father are getting the thanks they deserve," Mendez said. "This is theirs, not mine. They stood up against the establishment."

The school district in Berkeley, California, also celebrated Mendez. In 2018, the district renamed a public school the Sylvia Mendez Elementary School.

The legacy created by Mendez and her parents is still relevant today—many U.S. schools remain segregated for many reasons. Their dedication to equality is an important part of the fight to ensure equal access to education for all students.

Gonzalo and Felicitas Mendez Receive Recognition Too

Mendez's case would have never happened without the activism and dedication of her parents, Gonzalo and Felicitas Mendez. In 2000, a new high school in Santa Ana was named the Gonzalo and Felicitas Mendez Fundamental Intermediate School in their honor. In 2009, the Mendezes were also honored by the Los Angeles Unified School District. The district named a new East Los Angeles high school after them. It was named the Felicitas and Gonzalo Mendez High School.

GLOSSARY

agriculture (AG-rih-kuhl-chur)—growing crops and raising livestock

appeal (uh-PEEL)—the act of asking a higher court to review a case already decided by a lower court

boycott (BOY-kot)—to refuse to buy or use a product or service to protest something believed to be wrong or unfair

exploitation (ek-sploi-TAY-shuhn)—the act of using someone in an unfair or unjust way for selfish reasons

industrial (in-DUHSS-tree-uhl)—having to do with making things in factories

inferior (in-FEER-ee-uhr)—lower in rank or status

internment camp (in-TERN-ment KAMP)—a place where citizens are forced to live because they are seen as a danger during war

Latine (la-TEE-neh)—from or having ancestors from places in Latin America, such as the Dominican Republic, Mexico, and Puerto Rico

lawsuit (LAW-soot)—a disagreement that is decided in a court

outlaw (OUT-law)—to make illegal

precedent (PRESS-uh-duhnt)—a decision of the court from the past that judges and juries follow

segregation (seg-ruh-GAY-shuhn)—the practice of keeping groups of people apart, especially based on race

READ MORE

Hale, Christy. *Todos Iguales / All Equal: Un Corrido De Lemon Grove / A Ballad of Lemon Grove*. New York: Lee & Low Books, Inc., 2019.

Tonatiuh, Duncan. *Separate Is Never Equal: Sylvia Mendez & Her Family's Fight for Desegregation*. New York: Abrams Books for Young Readers, 2014.

Weston, Margeaux. *Brown v. Board of Education: A Day That Changed America*. North Mankato, MN: Capstone, 2022.

INTERNET SITES

Britannica Kids: Brown v. Board of Education of Topeka
kids.britannica.com/kids/article/Brown-v-Board-of-Education-of-Topeka/627788

Britannica Kids: Mendez v. Westminster School District of Orange County
kids.britannica.com/kids/article/Mendez-v-Westminster-School-District-of-Orange-County/633387/

Zinn Education Project: April 14, 1947: Mendez v. Westminster Court Ruling
zinnedproject.org/news/tdih/mendez-v-westminster/

INDEX

ABOUT THE AUTHOR

Leticia Gonzales was born and raised in Las Cruces, New Mexico. She studied journalism at the University of Minnesota. She also earned a master's in Human Services from Concordia University. Leticia lives in St. Peter, Minnesota, and she is the Assistant Library Supervisor at the St. Peter Library.